World Book's Learning Ladders

Earth's Features

WORLD BOOK

a Scott Fetzer company
Chicago
www.worldbookonline.com

WORLD BOOK

233 N. Michigan Avenue
Chicago, IL 60601
U.S.A.

For information about other World Book publications, visit our Web site at
http://www.worldbookonline.com or call **1-800-WORLDBK (967-5325)**.

For information about sales to schools and libraries, call **1-800-975-3250 (United States)**;
1-800-837-5365 (Canada).

Library of Congress Cataloging-in-Publication Data

Earth's features.
    p. cm. -- (World Book's learning ladders)
    Includes index.
    Summary: "Introduction to landforms and bodies of
water using simple text, illustrations, and photos.
Features include puzzles and games, fun facts, a
resource list, and an index"--Provided by publisher.
    ISBN 978-0-7166-7738-3
    1. Physical geography--Juvenile literature. I. World
Book, Inc.
GB58.E37 2011
551.41--dc22

                                      2010026718

World Book's Learning Ladders
Set 2 ISBN: 978-0-7166-7746-8

Printed in China by Shenzhen Wing King Tong Paper Products Co., Ltd.
Shenzhen, Guangdong
1st printing December 2010

Editorial
    Editor in Chief: Paul A. Kobasa
    Associate Manager, Supplementary Publications:
      Cassie Mayer
    Writer: Brian Johnson
    Researcher: Cheryl Graham
    Manager, Contracts & Compliance
    (Rights & Permissions): Loranne K. Shields

Graphics and Design
    Manager: Tom Evans
    Coordinator, Design Development and Production:
      Brenda B. Tropinski
    Photographs Editor: Kathy Creech

Pre-Press and Manufacturing
    Director: Carma Fazio
    Manufacturing Manager: Steven Hueppchen
    Production/Technology Manager: Anne Fritzinger

Photographic credits: Cover: © Dmitry Pichugin, Shutterstock; WORLD BOOK illustration by
Q2A Media; Shutterstock; p4, p6, p11, p12, p18, p26: Shutterstock; p8, p21, p22: Getty
Images; p9, p20: Alamy Images; p17: Masterfile; p23: SuperStock

Illustrators: WORLD BOOK illustration by Q2A Media

What's inside?

This book tells you about different kinds of landforms and how they shape Earth. You can also find out about bodies of water and their importance to people.

Mountain

A mountain is a part of the land that stands tall above the rest of the earth. Mountain peaks can reach into the clouds. The higher up a mountain you go, the colder it becomes.

Some mountains stand alone, but most come in a long row. Mountains that rise side by side are called mountain ranges.

The **peak** of a mountain may be covered by ice and snow.

The **slope** of a mountain may be steep.

Water from **snowmelt** flows down the sides of a mountain.

Forests cover the sides of most mountains. Trees do not grow on the peak.

It's a fact!
Mount Everest in Asia is 29,035 feet (8,850 meters) tall. That's as high as 23 Empire State buildings!

Mountain goats have large hoofs to help them climb steep slopes.

5

Volcano

A volcano is a place where hot liquid rock called lava flows out of the earth. Volcanoes also release ash and rocks. Some volcanoes give off lava slowly. Others explode in huge eruptions.

A volcano begins as an opening in the earth. Over time, dried lava or rock may build up around it. This gives the volcano its shape.

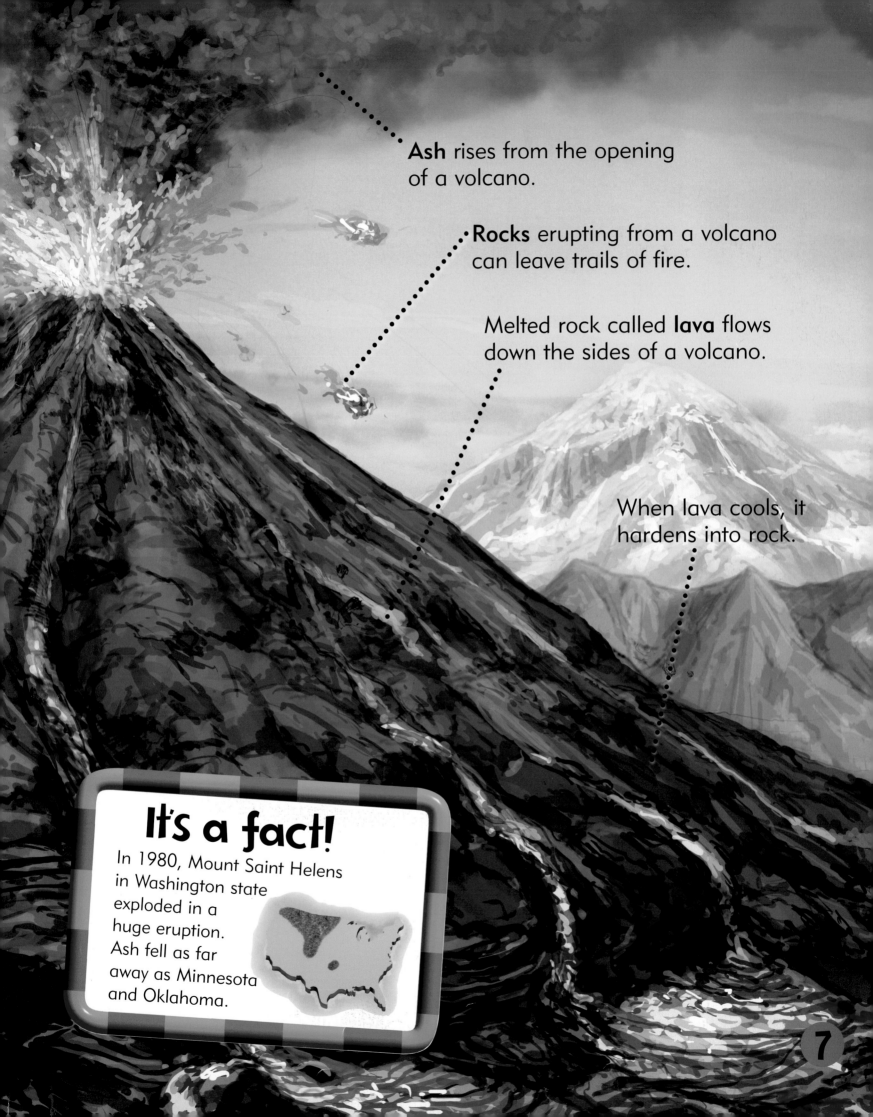

Ash rises from the opening of a volcano.

Rocks erupting from a volcano can leave trails of fire.

Melted rock called **lava** flows down the sides of a volcano.

When lava cools, it hardens into rock.

It's a fact!
In 1980, Mount Saint Helens in Washington state exploded in a huge eruption. Ash fell as far away as Minnesota and Oklahoma.

7

 # Cave

A cave has an opening called a **mouth**.

A cave is a naturally hollow area in the earth. The inside of a cave is a dark, damp place. Caves may have narrow tunnels and large rooms. Many caves are filled with hanging rocks that look like icicles.

Narrow **tunnels** lead to large rooms called chambers.

Most caves are made by **flowing water** that cuts through rock.

Some caves are made of ice. They are formed by streams that run under large areas of ice.

Stalactites hang from the ceiling of a cave.

Cavefish live in parts of the cave where there is no light. They cannot see, but they can feel even tiny movements in the water.

It's a fact!

Mammoth Cave in Kentucky stretches for more than 340 miles (550 kilometers). A horse would have to run for 11 hours to cover that distance!

Stalagmites form on the cave floor.

Plain

A plain is a broad, nearly flat stretch of land. Plains are often lower than the surrounding land. The grassy plain shown in the big picture is called a prairie.

Plains are mostly flat, with few mountains or hills.

Prairie dogs live together in burrows (underground holes).

There are few **trees** on prairies.

Tall grass grows on many plains.

The burrowing owl lives on the prairies of North America. It often nests in burrows that it steals from prairie dogs!

Wildflowers bloom on prairies.

Valley

A valley is a natural dip in the earth. Valleys run between mountains or across plains. Streams or rivers run through many valleys. Some valleys are narrow with steep sides. Others are wide with gently sloping sides.

Many valleys run between tall **mountains**.

Many valleys provide a path for **flowing water** to come down from mountains.

The bottom of a valley is called the **floor**.

Some people live in valleys. They may grow crops and raise farm animals along the floor or valley walls.

The sides of a
valley are called
valley walls.

It's a fact!

Death Valley is a hot desert valley
in California. The temperature
there has risen as high as
134 °F (57 °C)!

A valley may have rich
soil that is good for
growing **crops.**

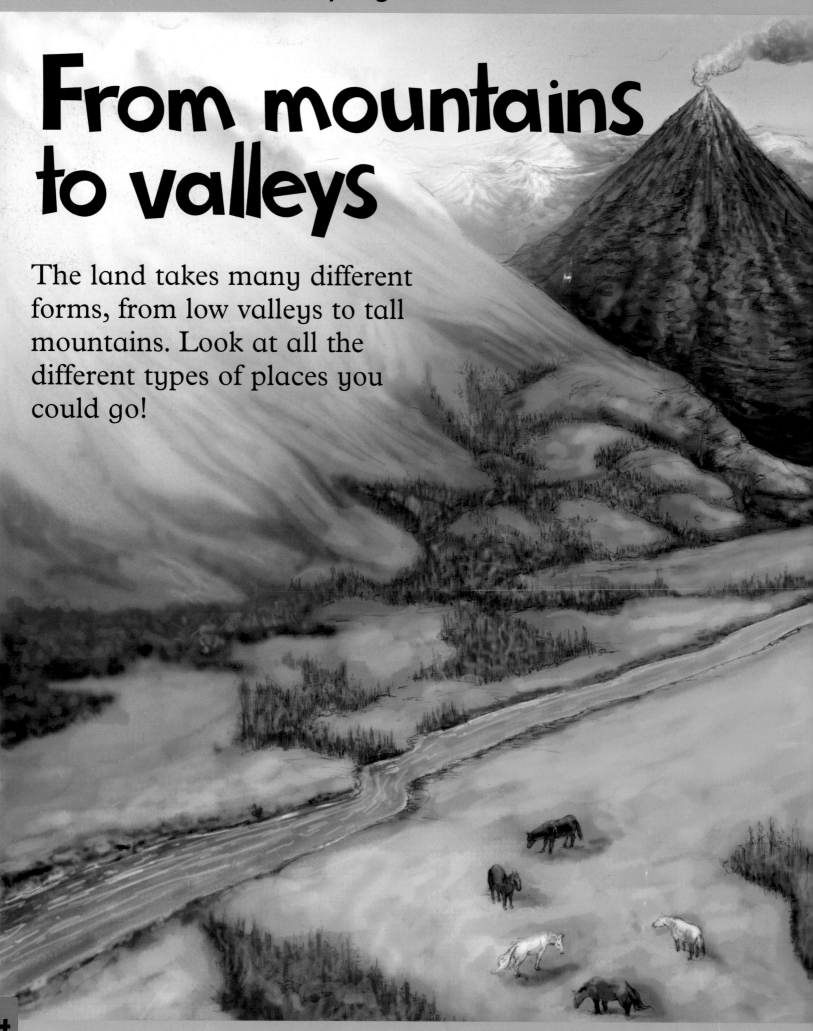

From mountains to valleys

The land takes many different forms, from low valleys to tall mountains. Look at all the different types of places you could go!

14

Where is the cave's mouth?

Words you know

Here are some words that you learned earlier. Say them out loud, then try to find the things in the picture.

ash   slope   floor
lava   snowmelt   mouth

15

River

A river is a large stream of water that flows over land. Most rivers begin on mountains or hills. Rivers flow downhill into other rivers, lakes, or the ocean. Almost all river water comes from rain or melted snow.

Trees line the **banks** of most rivers.

It's a fact!

The Nile River in Africa flows for 4,160 miles (6,695 kilometers). Even a speeding car would need three days and nights to drive so far!

Many rivers begin where **snowmelt** flows down from mountains.

A river cuts a **channel** through the land.

A river may spread out into a delta where it meets another body of water.

Some rivers have strong **currents**.

# Lake

A lake is a body of water surrounded by land. Some lakes are as large as seas! Most lakes are filled with fresh water. Fresh water is less salty than ocean water.

People have a lot of fun on lakes. These people are in a **sailboat**.

Most lakes are filled with **fresh water**.

The Dead Sea is a saltwater lake in southwestern Asia. It is so salty that people can easily float on top of the water!

Trees often grow along the **banks** of a lake.

When a stream reaches the edge of a lake, it may form a **waterfall**.

It's a fact!

Lake Baikal in Siberia reaches more than a mile deep. It holds more fresh water than all the Great Lakes of North America combined!

Ocean

The ocean is a large body of water that covers most of Earth. It is home to countless livings things. People depend on the ocean for food and for carrying goods to other parts of the world.

The ocean holds most of the water on Earth. It is made of **salt water.**

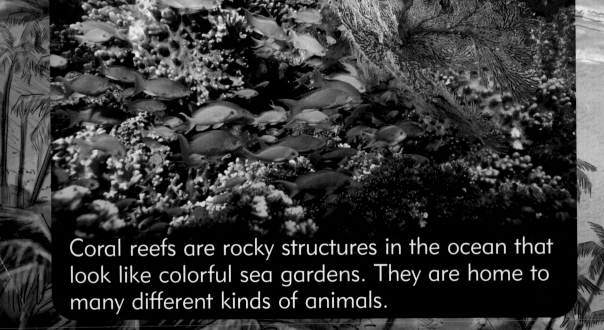

Coral reefs are rocky structures in the ocean that look like colorful sea gardens. They are home to many different kinds of animals.

Freighters carry the things that people make around the world.

Waves are caused by wind that moves across the top of the water.

In some parts of the ocean, a tall seaweed called giant kelp creates underwater forests.

Waves wash ashore onto the **sandy beach**.

Island

An island is a small body of land surrounded by water. Islands lie in oceans, rivers, and lakes around the world. New islands may rise when volcanoes erupt in the sea.

Many islands are mountains that rise from the sea floor.

Atolls are ring-shaped islands that are made out of the skeletons of ocean animals called corals. Plants and animals live on some atolls.

Some islands are made of **rock.**

Volcanic islands are formed by volcanoes under the sea.

Palm trees and other kinds of plants grow on islands in warm places.

Sandy beaches surround many islands. Sand is made of tiny bits of shell, rock, and other materials.

Rivers flow into the sea

Water shapes the land in many different ways. How many bodies of water can you find in this picture?

24

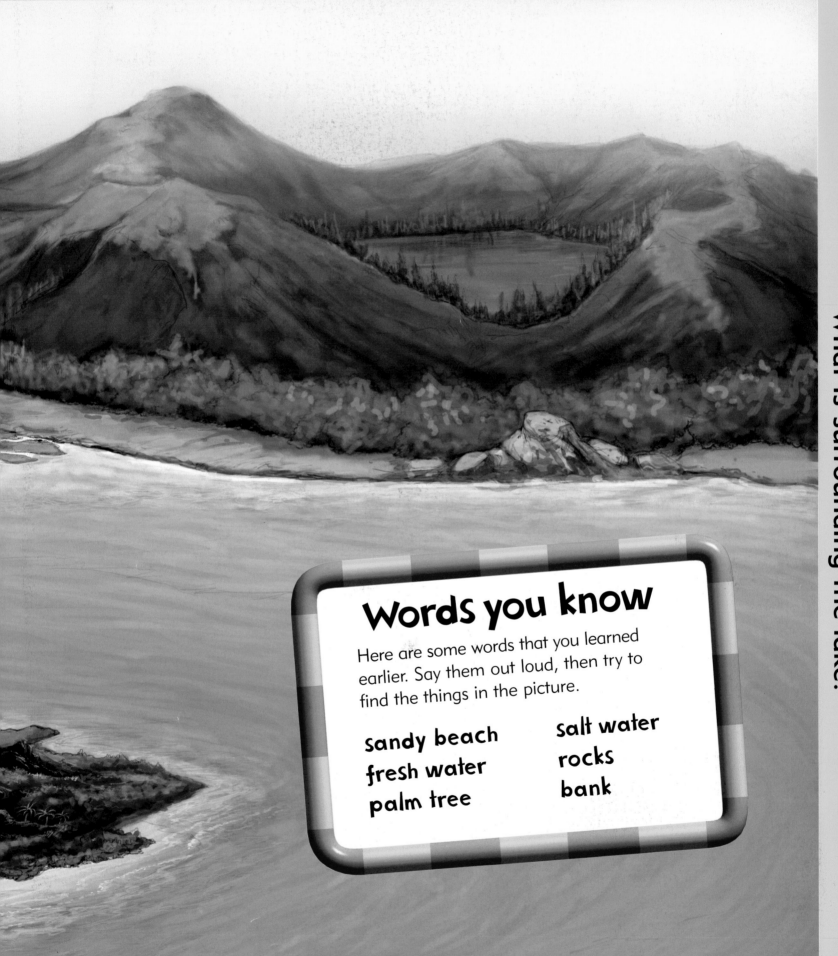

Words you know

Here are some words that you learned earlier. Say them out loud, then try to find the things in the picture.

sandy beach   salt water

fresh water   rocks

palm tree   bank

Did you know?

The Grand Canyon in Arizona is a deep valley with steep sides. It was formed over millions of years by a river cutting through soft stone.

About 97 percent of the water in the world is in the oceans. This means that most of the world's water is too salty for people to drink.

Between 50 and 70 volcanoes erupt every year. Many volcanoes are found in a "ring of fire" around the Pacific Ocean.

The air on top of mountains is so thin that people can hardly breathe. People who climb tall mountains bring air with them in special tanks.

SAM WAS HERE

The Amazon River in South America carries more water to the ocean than any other river. In some places, the river is so wide you cannot see the other side!

Ancient people left paintings of animals in hundreds of caves. One cave in France has paintings that are 32,000 years old!

Puzzles

Close-up!

We've zoomed in on three different features. Can you figure out which feature you are looking at?

1

2

3

Answers on page 32.

28

Double trouble!

These two pictures are not exactly the same. Can you find the five things that are different in picture b?

a

b

Match up!

Match each word on the left with its picture on the right.

1. beach

2. peak

3. stalactite

4. waterfall

5. lava

6. valley floor

a

b

c

d

e

f

Answers on page 32.

True or false

Can you figure out which of these statements are true? Turn to the page numbers given to help you find the answers.

Water in the oceans has almost no salt. **Go to page 20.**

3

1 Rivers flow from the oceans up into the mountains. **Go to page 16.**

The peaks of many mountains are covered by ice and snow. **Go to page 5.**

4

2 Many valleys have rich soil that is good for growing crops. **Go to page 13.**

5 Few trees grow on plains with grass. **Go to page 11.**

Answers on page 32.

Find out more

Books

The Highest Places on Earth by Martha E. H. Rustad (Capstone Press, 2010)
Learn all about places around the world with very high elevations.

Looking at Landforms by Ellen Mitten (Rourke Publishing, 2010)
How can lava form a mountain? How does weather shape the land? Read this book to find out!

The Lowest Places on Earth by Martha E. H. Rustad (Capstone Press, 2010)
Read this book to learn about places on Earth that are far below sea level.

Understanding Landforms by Barbara Taylor (Smart Apple Media, 2008)
This book will tell you all about mountains, volcanoes, rivers, and other features of the land.

World's Wonders: Landforms by Elizabeth Raum (Raintree, 2007)
Read this book and journey to amazing lakes, rivers, mountains and other natural wonders.

Web sites

Explore Mountains
http://www.mountain.org/education/explore.htm
Fun ways to learn about mountains, from the Mountain Institute.

Rivers and Streams
http://www.mbgnet.net/fresh/rivers/index.htm
The Missouri Botanical Garden takes a look at Earth's flowing bodies of water.

TerraWeb for KIDS!
http://terraweb.wr.usgs.gov/kids/
The U.S. Geological Survey Web site contains satellite pictures of Earth, fun facts about Earth, and "Cool Stuff to Do."

U.S.A. Games
http://www.sheppardsoftware.com/web_games.htm
Educational games that teach about the geography of the United States.

Answers

Puzzles
from pages 28 and 29

Close-up!
1. mountain
2. ocean
3. plain

Double trouble!
In picture b, the smallest palm tree and the shadow are missing, the sun is smaller, the birds are flying in the opposite direction, and the stripes on the sailboat are green.

Match up!
1. d
2. c
3. f
4. a
5. e
6. b

True or false
from page 30
1. false
2. true
3. false
4. true
5. true

Index